A LITTLE NORTH OF HOLLYWOOD

(Or, Dimly and in Flashes)

A LITTLE NORTH OF HOLLYWOOD

(Or, Dimly and in Flashes)

POEMS BY L.E.K. WILSON

THE POETRY PRESS
2009

HOLLYWOOD, CALIFORNIA

Published by
THE POETRY PRESS
of Press Americana

the press of

Americana:
The Institute for the Study of
American Popular Culture
7095-1240 Hollywood Boulevard
Hollywood, CA 90028

http://www.americanpopularculture.com

Cover Photo: c. 1920 publicity still of actress Norma
Talmadge, photographer unknown

Library of Congress Cataloging-in-Publication Data

Wilson, L.E.K.
A little north of Hollywood, or, Dimly and in flashes :
poems / by L.E.K. Wilson.
p. cm.
ISBN 978-0-9789041-7-3
1. Hollywood (Los Angeles, Calif.)--Poetry. I. Title. II. Title:
Little north of Hollywood. III. Title: Dimly and in flashes.
PS3623.I585463L57 2009
811'.6--dc22
2009030476

At the worst I accepted Hollywood with the resignation of a ghost assigned to a haunted house. I knew what you were supposed to think about it but I was obstinately unhorrified.

This is easier to say but harder to make people understand. When I was at Bennington some of the English teachers who pretended an indifference to Hollywood or its products really *hated* it. Hated it way down deep as a threat to their existence. Even before that, when I was in a convent, a sweet little nun asked me to get her a script of a screen play so she could "teach her class about movie writing" as she had taught them about the essay and the short story. I got the script for her and I suppose she puzzled over it and puzzled over it but it was never mentioned in class and she gave it back to me with an air of offended surprise and not a single comment. That's what I half expect to happen to this story.

You can take Hollywood for granted like I did, or you can dismiss it with the contempt we reserve for what we don't understand. It can be understood too, but only dimly and in flashes.

\- F. Scott Fitzgerald,
from *The Love of the Last Tycoon*

For Donly and his doorstep

Preface

These poems should not to be taken as autobiographical. Rather, they were written to reflect various points of view inspired by the people I have met while living and working in Los Angeles County. This book is about the dreamers, those who move to Hollywood to find and follow their calling. They are precious souls, noble and persevering. I hope I have been able to capture a few of their opinions, some of their experiences, and a little of their yearning, contradictory as it may be, at times hungry for success in the film industry, at times lonely for their hometowns, which, in many cases, have been decimated by the economy or natural disaster. The folks I have profiled here, then, are those who are caught, wedged as it were, just short of conquering their discipline, but with no real place to go home to. They're hanging on by their fingernails, sometimes determined to dictate their own destinies.

As F. Scott Fitzgerald reminds us in the epigraph to this poetry collection, Hollywood, and the people who populate it, may be understood "only dimly and in flashes." I think of each poem as a flash, dimmer perhaps than the bulbs of the ubiquitous paparazzi, but a light, nonetheless, illuminating a corner of the tender heart.

TABLE OF CONTENTS

I.

The Sweet Murder of These

Bar Nothing

Rita Hayworth simmered when she sang stripping off

one black satin glove after another her Gilda all

fire and frustrated desire flashing through red hair and

when she sat quiet her stillness so electric charged with

dark alleys and Johnny and the casino magic of Buenos

Aires one indiscreet affair then another smoldering

disappointment the defeat of distant drums and when

moonlight and candlelight failed their promise as well

she knew, just like Johnny said, a dollar is a dollar in

any language and ebony canes come with stiletto

daggers as Nazis lurk in shadows of seduction wrapping

her, him, all of them in the slick persuasive kiss of the

reptilian

411

I got a phone call from Cedars-Sinai
today. He said the doctor had come
into his room to apologize.

The doctor had told him he would live
to see his two sons grow up. But the
MRI told a different story.

The tumor, the one wrapped around
his brain stem, the one they had removed
in surgery a week ago, was only the top,
it seems, of something happening all
throughout his spine. A dandelion
explosion on top of a long stem.

He had gone to the emergency room
because of the headaches and that's when
they had found it.

He told me they were giving him dilaudid
so he could sleep. I said I heard some people
hallucinate when they take it.

A pause...

Maybe he could hallucinate a body, I said, one
whole and pink and clean. Like a bud, an
Alstroemeria bud, cool and fresh in its leaves.

Catalina Chopper Crash Kills Three, Injures Two

Tonight the company of that ill-fated helicopter

remains closed in memory of the pilot and the passengers. The helicopter crashed yesterday morning on the west side of Catalina Island. The pilot and two passengers were killed. Two other passengers were airlifted to Santa Monica Hospital where they remain in critical condition.

Witnesses say they saw flames coming from the helicopter before it dove into a field near Starlight Beach.

The names of the pilot and passengers have not been released pending notification of next of kin.

The NTSB is investigating the cause of the crash.

Embers

The first time you murdered me we were at a
bonfire on the beach you threw my bones in the
flames to erase any evidence the second time you
murdered me it was quieter less dramatic you had
my star pressed into Hollywood Boulevard then
you stepped on it every day on your way to work
one time you walked over it with your wife and I
looked up her skirt

Butterfly

You fluttered around my lemon
tree, alighting, white lace on yellow
rind. Your wings moved slightly in,
quivering, then still and sweet and
whisper quiet. My husband tells me
your lifespan is two weeks at the
most. I don't like this news and
wonder why the beautiful blinks
while the cruel yawns wide, so loud,
so long.

On Muses and Like Seductions

Fade In:

Act One

You walk in. Sit down at the table across from me. Smile. Flirt. You wear false eyelashes and fire engine lipstick because you know I can't resist that. You even go so far as to sip my favorite Pinot Noir.

Act Two

I fall for it and we begin again. You toss salads with baby greens and brew tea. Show me the tattoo on the small of your back. We go for long walks in Griffith Park. Salsa dance on the roof in nothing but moonlight.

Act Three

The Santa Ana winds blow hot and dry. I feel dizzy and nauseous. Lie down to take a nap. I wake up in time to catch the hem of your skirt as it disappears around the corner with the fireman who came to put out the brush fire. It's winter and, thanks to you, the chaparral on the hill has turned a brittle yellow.

Fade out.

Friday Night on Olvera Street

they string the paper lanterns humming plum
as the night sky dims and spiced sangria stirs
goblets late and strong

now the air heavy with cinnamon and sugared
churros bobbing in hungry hands while trumpets
pound a salsa tempo

here a ruffled dancer snaps her heels and twists
her chin away and over her bare shoulder so
haughty so high

and there in the kitchen a waitress pauses over
a burrito to open her compact and paint a
smile across her face

"So what do you do?" he had asked her.
"I'm an actress," she had said. "Oh yeah,"
his eyes open wide,

"which restaurant?"

Onion Powder

So I'm walking across the parking lot
and the guy on the bus told me it's 102
degrees but right now it feels more like

120 and I swear I can see oasis puddles,
heat waves squiggling over black tarmac,
like I'm fading into a dream sequence on

a 1950s television show. I tried to write
a television show but my mom told me
I couldn't make any money as a writer so

I got my own apartment on tujunga only
now I have to pay rent and food and gas
and electric (I had to let cable and phone

go) which brings me back to my journey
from the parking lot to coinstar, a bag of
change in a ziploc hidden in the backpack

banging against my hip like a neon sign,
"live nude girls," and I swear everyone's
staring at me but I know they're not, only

I can't believe it's come to this. All I have in
my kitchen is a jar of onion powder and a
bag of ice now my stomach's growling and

I'm starting to shake and the worst part
is I know there's only enough in the ziploc
to make it through tuesday so I'm not

sure what I'm going to do about wednesday
or thursday after that.

these are the bills that cannot be paid

i stack them by my microwave green and red
and yellow and blue they come by fours and
threes and twos these are the bills that cannot
be paid i douse them with my aftershave then
one by two by three by four i light the match
from the kitchen drawer these are the bills that
cannot be paid i dig out back a shallow grave then
blue then red then yellow then green I start all over
fresh and clean

The Hero's Journey

Trudging through wailing tundra I push green shoulders
slicing sharp wind pulling from magnetic pole strong like
snarling wolves who snap each heel with the persistence
of death while white snakes glide curve effortlessly

skimming sheets of ice spitting out forked tongues to
judge creation in ancient clarity daunting perpetual
motion like the phases of the moon inexorable while
needle rain pierces my eyes gutting all tears ice

wind singes my ears seals my lips steals my voice a
dark thief red and angry as the war drum the snakes
come still in tireless rhythm relentless hungry like
dusk who eats our days while I grab frozen breath to

slice forward another step from magnetic pole to
swallow sliver icicles straining toward the sun who
hides herself behind the western mountain so high so
dusted in arctic distance still the snakes suffer the

snow to cut like daggers the softest skin quiet stealthy
as the past and now I feel my bones groan crashing
against tired muscle the air cruel as smeared blood
until I stretch my mouth wide screaming in sacred fire

Mulholland Drive in January

The view from here in winter brings us to a study of
grays. The valley dusted in smog, a lighter shade like

that of a well-swept sidewalk. Then the San Gabriels, a
deeper shade like the fins of a shark. And the spiderweb

of boulevards and thoroughfares. They're somewhere
in the middle. Like the ashen faces I taped to my

bathroom mirror to help me keep things in perspective.
They stare at me across the decades through the dark

and dusty wires of Auschwitz as I, pitiful and morose
over a lousy audition, undertake my morning shave.

Skin Dirge in C Minor

I hate the word

    acne

A cacophony of consonants

    harsh and cruel

    like sand in crackerjacks

I wish for words like

    cream

    fresh, young, smooth

    like sweet tea on Sunday afternoon

But not to be

    for me

    inequitable

    acne

Movie Review

I once heard a critic say that she was struck by a great irony when she viewed the film *Citizen Kane*: the very tool that William Randolph Hearst had used to hurt so many others – the mass media – had been used against him. But

when I think about it now, that irony does not seem to me to be the central irony of the film. The central irony of the film is, rather, that the storyline follows less the life of Hearst and more the life of the filmmaker himself, Orson

Welles. It was Welles who grew up in a boarding school: his mother died when he was only nine years old, and his alcoholic father died but a few years later. Indeed, the filmmaker never really had a normal childhood, or a

childhood at all. When the banker comes to get young Kane in the film, and the boy's ties are severed from his parents, we know Welles is writing his *own* past. In that scene, the father seems angry, even abusive; the mother wants the

boy to be where the man can't hurt him. Could this be a subtle caricature of a devoted mother protecting a son from an alcoholic, abusive father? I can't stop thinking that it would be Welles who would hunger for a relic from the past, a relic of childhood, a time when he had both of his parents together, when he was happy, when he could simply play. Might that relic be...a bobsled? Hearst had a reputation for being cruel, but Welles too tore up people as

easily as he tore up rooms. A co-worker of the director once remarked, "You had to have a strong stomach because he was a genius, but he was a very difficult person to work with." When Kane destroys his wife's bedroom

after she leaves him, we are reminded of scenes from Welles's own biography. In one incident, the filmmaker felt RKO was foiling his plans, so he held an emergency meeting at a restaurant in Hollywood – he

didn't want his contract to expire without having made a film. At the meal, he got so angry with one of his compatriots he threw a flaming can of sterno at him. Another point of difference: Hearst never actually married

his actress-girlfriend, as Kane does in the film. And Davies never abandoned him. In fact, Marion may have been a gold-digger at first, but she eventually fell in love with the newspaper tycoon she called Pops. After the stock market crashed and Roosevelt instated income tax, the actress sold her jewelry and real estate to raise a million dollars to help her struggling lover. In later years, Welles confessed that he had been unfair to her in the film, that he regretted

the portrayal. Marion was nothing like Dorothy Comingore's character, the drunken and pathetic Susan Alexander, destroying Kane's political aspirations then leaving him. On the contrary, Hearst threatened to damage

Welles's reputation if *Kane* were released by exposing the filmmaker's affair with married actress Dolores del Rio, and Welles had a short-lived, tempestuous marriage with an actress, Rita Hayworth. In the end, Hearst died in the

home of Marion Davies, loved to the last. Welles, who had achieved great fame in his mid-twenties, lived a transitory life thereafter. Hopping around Europe, grossly overweight, running through several wives, piecing

together a living, Welles was miserable and commented in an interview near the end of his life, "I think I made essentially a mistake staying in movies...I would have been more successful if I had left...I have wasted the greater part of my life looking for money and trying to get along, trying to make my work...I've spent too much energy on things that have nothing to do with making a movie. It's about two percent movie making and ninety-

eight percent hustling. It's no way to live a life." To me, Orson Welles sounds beaten, bitter, and full of regret – just like that most well known of villains, Citizen Kane. Is it possible that therein lies the genius of the film: the

writer/director Welles (he shared an Academy Award with Herman Mankiewicz for best screenplay for *Kane*) was able to pull from his own life experience to find the innermost needs, desires, and regrets of a man, the

ultimate truth as he saw it? Or could it be that karmic justice fated the life of the filmmaker who some say brutally injured both Hearst and Davies? Or did the masterwork mesmerize and fixate the filmmaker to such a

degree that he had no choice but to play out the very life he had scripted?

Strike

A column published 12 February in Company Town

While I regret the result of the writers' strike, I get it. For those of you who don't have writer friends or live outside of the content-producing corridors of LA and New York, perhaps you don't know what I'm talking about, perhaps you haven't heard of a little Draconian clause written into all writer contracts: *force majeure*. Notice how quickly the

directors' contract was settled. Producers, networks, and studios know they can't go forward without directors. Even the ubiquitous game shows and reality shows need directors. But writers? The suits wouldn't negotiate with the writers because they needed the strike to last long enough for them to enact *force majeure*, or a severance of

contract due to extreme, unseen forces. A good old fashioned spring cleaning. Enacting *force majeure* allowed them to clear out the closets of the old model contracts they had with mature, seasoned writers. Rather than work with these folks on the New Media models, they swept them into a dustbin and threw them in the dumpster out

back. Dozens of contracts were cancelled and old deal writers "retired." While I embrace change, I also respect the years of work writers have spent perfecting their craft. This corporate downsizing – and make no mistake, that's exactly what it was – disrespects writing and writers alike. I was talking to a friend of mine who's a three-time Emmy

winning comedy writer. He reminded me that the networks and studios are now owned by billion dollar multi-national corporations. Entertainment is maybe 1-2% of their bottom line. They don't have any personal relationship with the writers like studio or network heads did in the Golden Age of Hollywood. Cutting all contracts in the six to seven figure range sounds really good to them. "Hey, get the kid to do it. Pay him peanuts." We all know someone who has been downsized no matter the industry. This fact of late twentieth and early twenty-first century corporate life denigrates the older and wiser among us for youth on the cheap. As long as suits continue to make this

decision, those same suits better not complain about quality. "Why are TV shows and movies so bad?" I often

hear people ask – suits included. "Because nobody cultivates and cares for the writing pool," I always reply.

Diner

2:30am. Friday night. And Bob's Big Boy on Riverside Drive is packed. Look around. Bikers crowd their black leather into the corner booth, Hollywood gals with Betty Page bangs lounge in the waiting area, as a crusty old comedian crunches toast at the bar, his personal assistant

hovering over his right shoulder. Amy, the waitress, rushes by with a steaming pot of coffee and scowls at the drunk producers blowing straw covers at two starlets seated at the counter. The parking lot overflows with cars as diverse as the patrons. An old Ford pickup in primer gray waits

beside a 2001 convertible Jag, its blue metallic and shining. "Democracy," John Russell Lowell whispers to us from the past, "is that form of society, no matter what its political classification, in which every man has a chance and knows that he has it." Does that definition of democracy still exist?

The homeless man, tonight huddled in a red parka on the bench across the street from Bob's, challenges us, haunts us. But in the American diner, we can glimpse the possibility of democracy, pure and true. Here, all races, all classes, and certainly both genders commune and break bread as one. The American diner may just represent the last place where all come together, if only for a chocolate shake, pancakes, and a slice of bubbling apple pie, and in that community find a reason to believe in the concept, at once elusive and illusory, known as *chance*.

Hotel Del

The historian of the hotel took us on a tour and spoke to us
of the western shore of Coronado Island where, as shining
as the Pacific, stands, all red turrets and chandeliers, the
historic Hotel Del Coronado. So few of the graceful old

hotels of the Victorian era have survived, yet somehow, by
the sheer force of her personality, the doors of the hotel
have not only remained open for over one hundred years,
he told us, they have been refinished as part of a welcome

restoration effort that insures she will continue to stand as
the "grand lady by the sea." It's 1885, he continued, and
Elisha Babcock and Hampton Story buy the undeveloped
Coronado Peninsula, subdivide it, sell off lots, and begin

building the hotel they hope will be "the talk of the
western world." It's 1888, the bottom drops out of the real
estate market. The very year the hotel opens its doors,
hundreds flee San Diego. But a private investor finances

Babcock and Story's project during those struggling years.
The market soon recovers, and the hotel finds herself a
favorite of wealthy Easterners looking for an alternative to
the East Coast and European travel. With World War I and

the institution of a personal income tax, he explained, the
hotel feared lean times once again, but her close proximity
to military bases actually sustained her through the Great
War. Officers on leave coupled with a booming stock

market kept a steady stream of guests flowing through the
Del's doors. Just as the hotel management was about to
breathe easy, the stock market crashed, and the hotel
found herself on the front steps of the Great Depression,

but somehow the Del was charmed once again. Hollywood, just a few hours north, came calling. The depression only increased film revenues, he stated, as many depressed Americans saved their pennies for a few precious hours of

happiness in a dark, cool theater staring at a silver screen. The Hollywood elite had more money than ever and came to the Del to spend it. Prohibition further helped the hotel as she found herself conveniently located between

Hollywood and Mexico where thousands flocked to buy booze and, he added, to gamble. World War II only increased hotel revenues as officers again found the resort a favorite for R&R, and the wartime economy

boomed. But after the war, the hotel fell on hard times. The survivors of the conflict were looking toward the future and the future meant *new*. They wanted new houses in suburbia, new cars, new appliances, and, yes, new resorts.

With the mass marketing of automobiles to the middle classes emerged a new fashion in resort living, the motor hotel. These new motels were designed for auto-owning families. They could drive up to a registration window,

much like fast food drive-through windows today, he supposed, and they could park right outside their rooms. The hotel, old and not so auto-friendly, was forced to rent rooms out yearly to boarders as if she were a rundown

apartment house and, he shuddered, she lost much of her earlier glamour. But fate would lend a helping hand once again. The Civil Rights Movement, the environmentalist movement, and the bicentennial celebrations of 1976

ignited a new interest in the history of our country and in preservation, he smiled. The Hotel Del once again found herself in fashion, and the recent renovation attests to the momentum she now enjoys. Another point of interest

keeps guests coming: the hotel is said to be haunted by the
ghost of Kate Morgan. In November of 1892, she checked
in alone and was soon after found dead of an apparent
suicide. Since then, several hotel guests have claimed to

see her roaming the halls or tugging at their bedsheets.
Perhaps one last factor has also helped the hotel's
popularity, he speculated. In 1958, director Billy Wilder
chose the location for his comedy *Some Like It Hot*, starring

Jack Lemmon, Tony Curtis, and the complicated Marilyn
Monroe. The American Film Institute ranked the film the
#1 comedy of all time and placed it at #14 on its best films
list. With these admirable rankings and the more recent

explosion of interest in film studies over the last twenty
years, he romanced, the hotel has a little Hollywood fairy
dust to add to its allure. To study the history of the Hotel
Del Coronado, he concluded, is to study the history of our

country. The hotel is not unlike the citizens that sleep
within her walls, he assured us. She is resilient and,
through even the worst times imaginable – recession, the
Great Depression, income tax, even war – she will survive.

Palm Springs

Harlow ordering breakfast at 3pm, Dali discussing the
relevance of his art and dismissing its scrutiny, Bogey
sunning by the pool. Wait, I know that voice, I'm sure it's

Mae West. And singing over there, that must be Sinatra. Liz
Taylor and Richard Burton in a fight... Do I see Howard
Hughes sipping a martini at the bar? Or is it only a mirage?

American Beauty

I hold a picture in my hand of a very young Katherine
Hepburn wrapped in a solid and simple black coat with her
hair parted cleanly on the side and brushed down, flat and
smooth, into a curved bob. She wears no jewelry and her

nails are short and unpolished. Eyebrows arch in calm
confidence while lips shine with the same wild intensity as
her ambition. A true American beauty. In 1855, Walt
Whitman published the first edition of *Leaves of Grass*. The

poem "Song of Myself" begins, "I celebrate myself" and
later commands, "You shall no longer take things at second
or third hand…nor look through the eyes of the dead…nor
feed on the specters in books, You shall not look through

my eyes either, nor take things from me, You shall listen to
all sides and filter them from yourself." This command to
develop a strong sense of self-identity, an intense self-
reliance, and to remain fiercely loyal to that sense cuts a

deep canyon through the American ethos. The nineteenth
century, we remember, also brought us Emerson, Thoreau,
and Dickinson, all encouraging us to think independently,
to be truly and completely ourselves. American beauty is

not as easy as donning chinos, a polo shirt, and loafers.
Indeed, it has nothing whatever to do with clothes. Rather,
it involves adopting a style that is completely and uniquely
our own, a style that shows the world we are comfortable

with who and what we are. Self-reliant. Independent. My
mind returns again and again to that photograph of
Katherine Hepburn not because of what she is wearing
or what she is not. My mind returns to that photograph

of Katherine Hepburn because of who she is. I see
passion, confidence, talent, intelligence in those eyes.
She knows who she is, where she is from, and, perhaps
most importantly, she knows exactly where she is going.

Film Festival

I imagine it's 1953, and I'm photographing a young Brigitte
Bardot posing in a bikini on the sand in front of the Carlton
Hotel. Or I imagine I'm lunching with Shirley Booth

wearing Chanel couture at the Miramar. Or I imagine it's
1970, and I'm holding Ottavia Piccolo's elbow as she
ascends the red-carpeted stairs up to the Palais des

Festivals. Later, I'll swing over to Cap d'Antibes and sip
Cristal until dawn at the Hôtel du Cap listening to Edith
Piaf sing "La Vie en Rose" (live). The next day, I'll buy a

diamond necklace at Cartier, try on bathing suits at nearby
Juan-les-Pins, and sun on a yacht just off the coast of the
Croisette. Who's that on the next yacht? Could it be

Bergman? Is he smoking cigars with, with Astaire? Could
be. And the biggest yacht? Why that's Mouna Ayoub's
Phocea, had lunch there yesterday. I'm in Dior shades and

the paparazzi, in black tie, are elbowing each other out of
the way to take my picture. Now I'm watching the sunset
from my suite on the top floor of the Martinez. Later, I'm

getting a massage and facial at the Givenchy Spa. Then I'll
pick up a little something at the Yves Saint Laurent
boutique to wear to dinner at Le Moulin de Mougins. Chef

Roger Verge is preparing the cuisine tonight. Darling, that
bauble you're wearing from Chopard is just divine. Did you
know they redesigned the Palme d'Or this year? It's an 18k

palm leaf mounted on a crystal base. Divine, darling. Just
divine. Yes, yes, darling. I have the all-access white pass.
Why Gilles Jacobs gave it to me, darling. Oh, you don't have

one. I'm so sorry, darling. Truly, I am. You wouldn't believe
how much I won at roulette last night at the Casino
Barrière. Oh yes, darling, Ingrid Bergman was there

playing blackjack. Yes, with Cary Grant. It's true. I saw
them myself. Yes, yes, I'm a star and you're a princess
sitting at a piano bar sipping Dubonnet with nothing more

pressing to do in the morning than make sure the Aston
Martin DB7 we have leased for the week has been polished
by the parking attendant to an Oscar worthy sheen.

Hollywood and Highland

I thought the worst the black fingernails peeling and
cracked but no the eyes faded dull scratched like marbles
flicked too many time from a boy's thumb onto steaming
concrete her cart parked by Marilyn's footprints in front of
Grauman's Chinese Theatre *You seen me in Sayonara* she
says *I'm one of the geisha they make them dancing girls but
they geisha everybody know censorship you couldn't even
show two married people in the same bed you should have
seen me in Sayonara my hair shiny black lips so red but quiet
red like the secrets of priests or stars and their plastic
surgery shhh* She pulls the lime green knit cap down under
her ears and picks her nose *I learned to dance in China* She
doesn't look Asian to me but I decide not to argue *I danced
in the circus we toured America and I hid in a locker at the
train station then I was on my own I didn't know my mom
and dad anyway I audition for the part get the part they love
me one time Brando kissed me behind my ear right here* She
taps her neck behind her ear with her cigarette hand as
ash falls on her shoulder like dandruff or lice *I a star big
star get a star here next month six weeks right here what
you think this good location* I look around and nod *I think
this a good location just waiting for Brando to call he call
real soon I stand here and wait for him to call you go away*

stand *you hanger's on key light key light move you in my key*

light I step back and watch her push her cart away one of

the wheels clicking like no cartilage bone on bone

Romancing the Villain

Don't expect white hats nor
white stallions neither only
poison stored in amulets
and knives hidden beneath
chaps sometimes coyotes
howl to announce us or
sometimes slink in behind
as the scarlet sun sinks on
the horizon and the boy only
ten wants to believe, but we'll
take his daddy's cattle too and
siphon the water from their
land as the bloodthirsty winds
heave and seethe their way
across the dry river bed.

An American in Sunglasses

1961. Paramount Pictures releases the film adaptation of

Truman Capote's 1958 novel *Breakfast at Tiffany's*. Audrey

Hepburn, cast as the film's leading lady Holly Golightly,

delicious in her simple black gowns, broad brimmed hats,

strands of pearls, diamond tiaras, and, just like Jackie,

enormous sunglasses. I wear pink lipstick, keep perfume in

my mailbox, and adopt stray cats. I hum "Moon River" and

ask people what a "huckleberry friend" is. I draw the line

at shoplifting. But remain true to the notion of marrying a

slightly cracked, yet incredibly urbane, young novelist.

No

it's more like the air in an

empty jar, a vacuum, an absence, a

black hole

never formal letters never

phone calls

a simple seeping with time a

slow dawning

like Zyklon B sprinkled in the barracks

quietly eating the air while hammers

nail the doors and windows shut

F. Scott Fitzgerald

EXT. SUNSET BOULEVARD - GARDEN OF ALLAH – NIGHT

A Spanish style apartment complex.

INT. BUNGALOW LIVING ROOM

Sparse décor. Not posh. Not even comfortable. A desk. A couch. A coffee table.

On the coffee table, a bottle of gin, a bottle of cola.

F. SCOTT FITZGERALD (late 30s), in shirt-sleeves, a tie, sits at his desk typing on his Underwood. He is sweaty, disheveled.

A pack of Chesterfield cigarettes rests on the desk beside the typewriter. One burns in an ashtray.

Fitzgerald stops. Reaches for the cigarette. Takes a drag.

He turns, looks at the bottle of gin, turns back to the Underwood. He continues to type, cigarette dangling from his lips.

He stops, stands, paces, rolls up his sleeves, smokes the Chesterfield.

He walks toward the bottle of gin. Stops. Smokes. Bends and reaches for the cola.

He returns to the desk, puts the cigarette in the ashtray, swigs the cola. Types.

He stops typing, turns, looks at the bottle of gin. Returns to the cigarette and the cola. Alternating a swig and a drag. A swig and a drag. He puts both down.

He types. Then stands, hands in hair, pacing.

He walks to the bottle of gin with sudden purpose, picks it up, grabs his suit jacket and a hat. Exits through the front door.

Casablanca

She went to film school and wrote a very important and influential thesis which can be summarized as thus: Light glitters seductively from an empty champagne glass while a strong hand toys with a white pawn belonging to a

handsomely inlaid chess set and a cigarette balances on the edge of an already overcrowded ashtray. A few moments earlier, a white slip of paper had appeared, obsequiously asking permission that one thousand francs

be paid to some anonymous and fortunate party. In bold letters, with a thick black grease pencil, the chess player's hand temporarily abandoned the white pawn to write, "O.K. Rick." And now, silently, the smoke from the cigarette

curls upward, the hand reaches for the cigarette and brings it up to the lips, and the camera follows. Here, for the first time, we see Rick. In Hal B. Wallis's production of *Casablanca*, director Michael Curtiz delays the appearance

of Humphrey Bogart's character, Rick, a full twenty-four shots from the moment the arriving German plane flies behind the sign for Rick's Café Americain. This sign is shot from a low angle, with nothing but the sky and the plane carrying German officials in the background, implying that this is a sign for an important place run by an important man. Ten shots later, the German officer Major Strasser descends the stairs of the plane to meet Captain Renault of

the local police. The Major inquires about the suspect who killed two German couriers in order to obtain the exit visas they were carrying. The Captain assures him that there is no hurry, for the suspect will be at Rick's that night,

"Everybody comes to Rick's." To which the major replies, "I have already heard about this café and also about Mr. Rick himself." Thirteen shots later, we get our first look at our hero's face, and this artful use of slow disclosure enshrines

Rick at the very nexus of American, patriarchal, imperialistic, white power. Now let's look closely at those next thirteen shots to see how Curtiz achieves this effect. The first shot is a high angle establishing shot of the front

of Rick's Café Americain. Following this is a low angle close-up of the sign we had seen in the sky, but this time it's lit up in neon shining boldly in the night. The image takes up the entire screen, which leaves no room to doubt the importance of the café. Next, a tilt shot brings us down from the close-up of the sign to the doorway of Rick's. Slowly, the camera dollies in the door, and we feel like patrons walking in. The establishing shot was from the left

side of Rick's, so the dolly-in swings us first to the front and then inside as if we were walking down the street from the left and took a left to enter Rick's. This subjective shot technique makes us part of the atmosphere, one of the

patrons, one of the masses. Not Rick. Once we are inside the club, the film cuts to a dolly shot that is taken from the left side of the room scanning the length of it from right to left. Stopping on Sam, the black piano player, the

camera slowly moves in for a close-up. This dolly shot acts much as a master or establishing shot would. It shows us the room, the people, the tables, the waiters, the ubiquitous cigarette smoke, and Sam. All of Rick's

kingdom, all of his domain, all at his command. After the close-up on Sam, a colored face that clearly works for Rick, the film cuts to a medium shot of two Moroccans wearing fezzes and smoking from a hookah. The next series of shots reveals the desperate situation of many while Rick, we later realize, sits coolly and calmly above the fray, indeed, even playing a game. From the Moroccans, Curtiz pans left stopping on two old men smoking and complaining that

they will never get out of Casablanca. Next, a middle-aged woman selling her diamond bracelet, probably a family heirloom, takes much less for it than what it is worth. The third shot in this series contains two old men whispering

secrets then falling silent as a German officer walks by. Lastly, two men discuss plans to escape by boat in the morning. These four medium shots only last a few seconds each, yet they rapidly tell us that these people have

problems with money, German officials, visas, transportation; in short, they face difficulty and danger. In addition, they forestall our introduction to Rick heightening our suspense and his mythic stature. From the

two men discussing their plans for escape, the camera pans, again following the movement of a waiter, to a man sitting at the bar having a drink and talking to the bartender. This medium shot stops with the bartender,

Sacha, on center screen, just as the earlier camera movement stopped on Sam. Again, a colored face works for Rick. Cutting to the head waiter, Carl, not a person of color but still a foreigner, Curtiz introduces us to the third

significant employee at Rick's, but we still have not seen Rick himself. A tracking shot follows the head waiter as he walks into the back gambling room; the film then cuts to a close-up of two attractive females inquiring about the

elusive Rick. The head waiter explains to them that Rick never drinks with patrons, a comment that further elevates his status. A few shots later, the film cuts back to the front room as a swarthy waiter approaches a table

with a white slip of paper in his hand. The camera is on the right side of the table, and in the bottom right hand corner of the screen we see an arm in a white dinner jacket lying across the table. The waiter is centered in a medium shot,

and the arm crosses the bottom left hand corner of the screen. The arm takes the paper, and we now arrive at the scene with which we began. Cutting to an extreme close-up of a check requesting payment of a thousand francs, Curtiz tells us two things: first, this mystery man has a great deal of money at his disposal; second, this mystery man must grant permission for things to happen. As the hand signs "O.K. Rick," we wait impatiently for a glance at such an

important person. Curtiz cuts to the front of the table in a close-up of the champagne glass, the left side of the chess board, the ashtray, the hand toying with the pawn, and we are left wondering what kind of man drinks a lot (the glass

is empty) of an expensive beverage (champagne) and plays the intellectual game of chess alone in a crowded room. As the hand reaches for the cigarette and brings it to the lips, the camera tilts upward, and we see the face of Rick for the

first time in a quintessential display of slow disclosure. Steadily, the camera pulls back from the close-up of Rick to a medium shot as we watch him move (predictably I might add) the white knight. Curtiz adroitly controls the images

on the screen and their sequence mixing mystery, suspense, desire, each a separate strand woven together like the three strands of hair in a little girl's braid. By the time we see Rick, we fully subscribe to his mythic stature, and the American, patriarchal, imperialistic power structure is comfortably secure. The white American male runs a café stocked with foreign personnel. He alone, omnipotent, controls money, women, Sacha, Carl, Sam,

even Captain Renault. So strong is he, in fact, that there is no opponent worthy of him. Thus he sits alone in a white dinner jacket and a black bow tie drinking champagne, smoking cigarettes, and playing *himself* in a game of chess.

Screenwriter

Journal Entry

1 March

The bitter rain of winter has stopped pounding Hollywood now, and the icy wind that slices through the Angeles Crest Mountains has given way to a warmer, whispier one off the

Pacific. Perfect walking weather. I started south on Highland, took a right on Paul Newman, and continued west on the Walk of Fame. Taking special care to

pirouette over both Fred Astaire and Ginger Rogers, I followed discarded pages from *Variety* and *The Hollywood Reporter* as they landed first on Valentino then Gene

Kelly, finally nestling into Lana Turner's footprints in front of Mann's Chinese. The smell of hotdogs from a nearby vendor drifted by me as "Isn't It Romantic?" swelled

vaguely from a speaker across the street. From here, I had an excellent view of the golden dragon rising from red flames above the entrance to the theater. I stared at that image awhile, imagining that the dragon looked like a demon writhing in the pit of hell and wondering about the metaphorical implications of that fact here in the heart of

Hollywood. But never mind that now. A sudden gust swept the discarded pages out of Lana Turner and, as if the gust had ordered those pages to dance, they waltzed toward

the El Capitan Theatre. I found myself chasing them down like an actor chasing down the casting calls printed on their pages. Then they disappeared, vanished, floated

above the rooftops like so many other Hollywood dreams, and I was left alone to wonder why the pages of *Variety* and *The Hollywood Reporter* had brought me here to the

front doors of the El Capitan. So I looked down and read the name off the star at my feet. I guess fate was trying to inspire me, but maybe fate never read any Harold Bloom.

Monument Valley

we drove north on Highway 163 toward the Arizona-Utah
border and finally got caught by sunset no luck seeing the
landscape in the late shades of day we had driven into a
bottle of black ink and couldn't see past our headlights

but now that I think on it maybe that's the best way to
enter the valley cause in the morning when we pushed
up the shades on our camper we felt like we'd just
walked into a surprise party filled with confetti and

champagne suddenly buttes and mesas thin and broad
rose up from the desert floor striping the sky as turquoise
as the stones encrusting the silver jewelry sold from the
nearby stands to think we had ignorantly passed these

very formations hidden in the dark and had no more
knowledge of their existence than we had knowledge of
the deepest Pacific and the color of these monuments a
shade of rose so subtle they've never been accurately

captured on film here we were in Ford Country I hoped
we'd see the ghost of John Wayne gallop by on a white
horse but no such luck only the Battle of Wounded Knee
two rattlesnakes and poison water in a rusty canteen

Sunset Boulevard

celluloid slips through my fingers silvery ships
dreaming film festivals a cigarette on Garbo's
lips champagne in fluted crystal as four seasons of
mirrors lilies white roses chiffon gowns and

smog hangs over Stanwyk's star a venomous
liquor promising box seats and backstage theater
only abscessing Sodom veins scarred the deep
purple of royal excess of sushi sharp knives and

red carpets with black velvet ropes diamonds
dripping from the whitest throat top hat tails
tango on black marble floors the piano plays
Cole Porter under an imported chandelier and

bums piss vodka lost in Clark Gable's mustache a
winter rain mud and monsoon drowns her
audition head heavy with stardust only one more
and the gilded door arabesque swings on hinges of

inlaid chess boards the queen imperial jade a
carriage of eighty chestnut stallions proud with
arched neck and chrome highly polished under
moonlight that softens the sweet murder of

these

II.

Homesick

The Attic

I remember falling from that ladder the smudge
of pink on the ribbon of a Degas ballerina and my
grandmother's bone china on the hutch her pattern
green bamboo with gold tipping the ladder a trendy
substitute for stairs to a loft and an attic door and as
I moved backward through space and I often wish
time I see the Queen Anne chair with cream brocade
and the dim halo of a lamp heavily shaded and on
the bookshelf as it whizzes past me I read John-Paul
Sartre *Being and Nothingness* just before I hit the
ledge and hear the snap of cracking ribs.

Tadpole

Crouching on a sandbar, I trace the tadpoles, hundreds,
in their static wiggling motion, they take over a tiny jetty
in this creek at the bottom of the hill, but also, without
real direction, without a discernible purpose or goal, like
so many bumper cars when the fair comes to the dry and
dusty field just outside of town, crashing, twisting,
refusing to heed direction from the steering wheel,
the driver, red lights flashing then green, and the horn
of clown cars, a two headed snake, the bearded lady,
elephant ears, hey lemme guess your weight, and yet, and
yet, the boys splashing at the far end, down by the bend,
create a wake, a new current which nudges a larger
tadpole, already growing four legs, onto the sandy bank,
these her first steps on shore, I press my pinky into the
sand right in her path, she steps onto my finger, I lift her
up and stare into those fresh black eyes and hope within
the chaos, always this force of change, this intention.

Hurricane

the sun gold as candlelight turning to pearl the powdered
sand on my toes and now a seagull screeches death as
maggots consume crab cadavers a dumpster reeking fish
skeletons the lime green of frothy margaritas and clearest
sky the color of hyacinth in May as sandcastles praise a
childhood in storybooks while blackest cloud threatens
flood a choking rain thick like sewage flushing split houses
into a bay as pure as summer's blonde hair flying through
white breeze shrimp cocktail chilled on balconies of finest
alabaster shimmering in moonlight buried now in tempest
sludge cracked like ancient tombs wind wailing stories of
shattered memory and dusk brings stars as bright as
sunburnt shoulders turning for the first kiss as waves
relentless and eternal promise fried mullet and raw
oysters sour and poisonous as thieves.

Quiet, like Smoke

her secrets floating through naked trees behind her
once home now swirling rubble a wooden spoon a
scrap rag of velvet curtain vermillion like the blood of
her son now missing three verminous days of salt
water soaked blueberry muffin and water moccasins
coiled in fruit baskets poisonous as the wicked
witch of the wind whipping the sea into vengeful
surge she turns and in her eyes I see reflected the

gulf
now quiet, like smoke

gumbo ya-ya

sure i'll show ya my secret come on in this here

kitchen you gonna need bout four five big pieces of

chicken salt n peppa then dust em with a little

flour just like this mmhmmm course i do who

wouldn't love it coffee and chicory on sunday

morning red beans and rice on monday dribble a

little oil in the cast iron skillet that's right you're

doin real good course i had their beignets who

hadn't piled high with powder sugar mmhmmm now

take that there chicken out no ma'am don't you clean

that skillet gotta make you roux just get you some

flour there's more in that tin you gonna need

you a wooden spoon it's right here hon i know

your kitchen better n you do okay now

sprinkle that flour and stir til it looks like hot

chocolate course not that carriage too rich for

my blood but i did think it seemed real nice

sittin under a blanket clop-clop on cobblestone

like a fairy tale scuse me lemme dice this

here onion and while I'm at it the chicken too no

never had a portrait done jackson square's

for tourists cept the bums that sleep in the

storefronts at night guess they're locals okay

now stir in this onion watch it don't burn

yourself. fema? please child don't bother me

with that nonsense now the celery and bell

peppers we gotta let that simmer for a minute or

two soften up why a hurricane's just light and dark

rum grenadine orange juice some folks maybe drip a

little passion fruit in there or some simple syrup but

you absatively have to garnish it with an orange

slice and a cherry wouldn't be the same without

it. the most? i probably miss the crawfish the jazz

"body and soul" definitely my favorite the magnolias

in full bloom the black curls of a wrought iron

balcony sure i will we'll do jambalaya on friday

and etouffe sometime next week now we gottta

sprinkle in some garlic cayenne oregano good now

this here basil thyme bay leaves I sewanee here

taste mmhmmm that's gonna be a mighty fine batch maybe

a little more salt n peppa stir in that broth mmhmmm

that looks real nice can you hand me that i diced up

some sausage this afternoon stir that in and the chicken

too no can't say i do last time i was on bourbon street

some college kid vomited on my alligator pumps no

S irree didn't like that one bit not yet you gotta

sprinkle in this here fil powder now you're done just

gotta let it simmer for hours or thereabouts i done

told ya didn't have a car if they're gonna order you

out they gotta come getcha yeah houston's okay

but no matter how far i go just can't get it out of my

head me on the rooftop and floatin past that big body

all bloated and blue

Chipped Fingernails

No, actually, I learned about the war from
watching my mother. These were the rules:

One

If the phone rings after ten or before nine,
don't answer it. If you touch the phone, you
will hear your name screeched to the heaven's
so loud, they will hear it on the space shuttle.
Only mom can answer the phone ten pm to
nine am. (Hand shaking. Voice the same. Face
white as the corn starch she uses to thicken
her gravy.)

Two

If anyone comes to the front door in a uniform,
you are absolutely not to answer it. If you touch
the door knob, you will be grounded until next
Christmas. Not this Christmas, next Christmas.
I don't care if it's UPS. If a man comes to that door
with a uniform, only mom can answer the door.
(Chewing her thumb. Robe clutched tight at
her neck.)

Three

You may never, ever watch anything about it
on television. Never. Ever. If you happen to
flip past a channel and see it, you must change
the channel right away. Absolutely no exceptions.
Especially if your little sister is in the room. Do
you understand me young man? (One day I got

home from soccer practice early and there
she was on the couch watching CNN and this
one clip of a dead soldier on a dusty Iraqi
street. She just kept rewinding it again and
again trying to get a good look at his face. Chipped
fingernails. Black roots. Already a glass of wine death
gripped in her fist.)

Foreclosure

All the houses empty on my
street. The windows broken
out. Grass knee high. I'm two
months behind and just got
laid off at the plant. I'm not
really interested in hope. I
just need a job.

Night Shift

"I can't stay up that late."

"It's all I've got."

"I've got two kids."

"So do I."

"Do you have any kind of daycare, nightcare, whatever?"

"Like a nursery?"

"Yeah."

"No benefits."

"Not even health insurance?"

"No benefits."

"Haven't you got anything else?"

"It's all I've got. Do you want it or not? I got ten people behind you."

"Alright. I'll take it."

"Okay. Sign here."

State Tax

There's an $800 alternative
minimum tax doesn't matter
if you make money, break
even, lose money that's why
folks are moving out of the
state they get behind and
late fees and then they owe
$4000 before they know it
and they can't ever catch up
so they move to Florida

no state tax

Repo Man

But how will I get to work? I can't afford a bike. Just give me one more week. Don't you see that kid in there? What will I tell him? How will I get to work? I haven't got it. If I had it, I would give it to you. What, you think I'm holding out on you? Look at this place. Can't you see there ain't no money? I'll give you a hundred bucks. It's all I've got. Except a little. You have to leave me with a little. I have to feed that kid in there, right? Right?

Addict

A green field. And a yellow daisy. We lie down and stare at
the sky. That cloud looks like a lollipop with a salamander

tail, you say. I disagree and say it looks like an electric
guitar. I ask you to pass it to me. You do. I smoke it. Then I

tell you we should go to Long's Drugs to buy the stuff to
make it with. Just do it ourselves. Save money. Be careful,

you say. You know a girl who blew her hotel room clean
out. I tell you to shut up. She's stupid, I say, not smart

like me.

Flying in for the Funeral

Above the clouds soft and crumpled
and white like a laundered cotton
sheet fresh from the dryer. The sky
slate blue. A gibbous moon luminous,
high. No birds up here. No life at all.

Quiet and clear. Like heaven. Scored
by the dull hum of a jet engine.

Pastrami on Rye

(This is what Father Frank said to me over pastramis at the deli.) *Certain places we can't forget. We need them. We crave them. We drink them up.* (Kitten soft and cocoa warm, I said. He nodded.) *When the Santa Anas blow prim and primordial. When Malibu Canyon seethes with flame and ash. When hope fails us and rejection presses down. We can scarcely rise from our beds. The nerves. Worn, raw. We tilt the key light on these moments, flashes from our past. Life jackets, respirators. Climbing over the low stone wall to pick apricots. Taking the first dive from the high board at the neighborhood pool. Sipping mom's homemade lemonade on the oak swing with Annie. Just sixteen. These, the familiar, the comfortable. They steady us for the steep and rocky climb. Like God and prayer and angels. Green and iridescent. Spinning through our daydreams.* (I told him he missed his calling. He should have been a poet. He laughed, lifted a glass of red wine.) *The blood of Christ.* (He took a sip.) *Strength for the journey.* (I bowed my head and thought "amen.")

L.E.K. Wilson is a poet living in Southern California. She teaches writing at Pepperdine University in Malibu where she has also directed the MFA program. She edits the creative writing journal *Review Americana* and holds a Ph.D. in American literature and film studies from the graduate university at The Claremont Colleges.

www.ingramcontent.com/pod-product-compliance
Lightning Source LLC
Chambersburg PA
CBHW031328060726